The Art of the FlockCall;
Creating your Successful Companion Parrot Lifestyle

By Kathy LaFollett

An introduction.

Parrots are a wonder. Every moment I share with my flock, or work with another's flock there is a moment of awe found. They are without doubt companion, not pet. Companion Parrots offer a relationship that has no comparison in challenge or magic. They help us to be better people, if we allow them.

They elevate our own awareness and empathy, if we allow them. They heal a saddened heart, uplift a low spirit and share our life's moments of simple joy. At every turn in their company I am in awe of their sincere and intelligent conversation. I write for people currently sharing their life with companions, for those hoping to share their life with a companion, and for the parrot curious wanting to learn.

Success with a companion parrot is not found in the parrot, but in the human in the room. Unreasonable expectations based on false self-awareness is the epicenter of failed parrot relationships. The art of creating a successful companion parrot lifestyle first starts in the human heart. Our Companion Parrot is a mirror into our own true character, and the companionship created makes us better humans. The core belief in my advocacy; Companion Parrots are not pets. They are cognizant, thinking, assessing, empathetic and emotional free thinkers. Companion Parrots choose through opinion and instinct. They are fully aware of their place and situation. Companion Parrots are an elevated species in all sizes, colors and personalities that deserve their equal share of understanding and respect inside the human dynamic.

It is my advocacy mission to remove the word "pet" from the vocabulary referring to parrots. I write this book to open up the dialogue necessary to walk down the roads required to make this first simple goal a reality. I write to celebrate the incredible joy and celebration of love and loyalty a parrot brings to anyone's lifestyle.

The ideas put forth here will help you create a deeply personal, satisfying and loving Companion Parrot Lifestyle with your feathered companion. Parrots are not complicated. Companion Parrots and their care is a straight forward requirements list. I have a library full of information on their requirements and care at FlockCall.com. Sharing your world with a Companion Parrot is not complicated. Unless you make it so, and I will show you how to keep this all very simple. And that will leave time and room for the joy, calm and confidence we all want in our personal Companion Parrot Lifestyle.

There is not another comparable relationship experience for a human like that of a companion parrot. They are as close to magic beans on earth as any fairy tale has told. Choosing a parrot is choosing a friend who can fly. Consider that for a second. What kind of personality would you be, if you could fly? Would you be confident? Would you be certain? Would you rely on that super power to evade problems or get to interesting things quicker? What and who would you be if you could fly?

You would be magic beans to start. Add to your super powers the ability to communicate, problem solve, understand your surroundings and have an opinion and you've got a bag of magic beans on a unicorn! Which is why I say with confidence there is not another companion animal anywhere that can be compared to parrots. Not one. I have shared my life with just about every available companion considered appropriate. I cannot think of one creature that has brought me more joy, insight, retrospect and personal growth as a person than my 8 birds. Each of them brings me their personality, preferences and choices. Each has their own sense of humor and confidence. Every single bird requires a relationship model from me specific for them. And yes, they are exactly like a 3-5 year old child in intellect and problem solving. I've had a couple of those for comparison as well.

I should warn you now, follow these ideas with confidence and calm and your success will create a situation where you may just be a happier, kinder and more peaceful person, with a parrot! I can say that because you cannot fool a companion parrot, they know when we are pretending. And a companion parrot will reject all obfuscation, falsehoods and tricks. Sincerity is required to create a relationship with a Companion Parrot.

Chapter 1
Know Thyself and Acknowledge that Truth

"What kind of bird do you think I should get?" I find myself answering that question quite often.

The question reveals a missed step. Know thyself. The inquiring person hasn't taken a good hard look at their life, their available time, their habits, or tendencies. It's who *we* are that really matters when choosing a parrot.

My answer to this question is always the same, "What kind of life do you live now?"

The inevitable answer back; "Well, I wasn't thinking of it that way. I was thinking I wanted a bird that doesn't bite, will learn to talk and do tricks, and go places with me!"

"OH!" I say. "Well that first bit is impossible."

You may already have companions in your home, this thought process can help reveal causes to problems that may have sprouted up lately between you and your companion.
Reflecting on our personal truth with honesty helps to understand the struggles of companion parrots inside the human dynamic. If you are considering adding a new companion to your current flock, this type of lifestyle review is important. Know thyself. Know thyself as you are right now as your home and family are currently. Do not romanticize what "it would be like" because it never is. It will be what it is and what you are right now, but with a parrot. Be honest with yourself. If you are always rushed for time, if you are a type "A" personality prone to control issues and always striving, if you see life as a field to do a career on; Get a houseplant. Companion Parrots aren't a good partner for people who focus only on tomorrow and themselves. You have to be in the here and now sharing all with a focus on them and you both, as a flock.

You are who you are and getting a parrot won't change that. Be honest with yourself. We are all different and have our own ways.

Sometimes, our ways are completely diametrically opposed to the true needs of a Companion Parrot. Realize a parrot does not do well under certain situations with certain personality types. It is no different between people in relationships. Some are meant to be, some were never meant to be. The difference between human relationships that don't work and human-parrot relationships that don't work is parrots have zero control over what happens to them after the relationship fails. They are at the mercy of the broken relationship and human wanting out. Statistically, the parrot suffers homelessness or being passed around from home to home.

There is a man who owns a Grey. He is a very controlling personality, very certain about his opinion. He shoves his hands under his bird's belly quickly and demands, Step Up! He moves too fast. Greys do not do well with that at all. Greys are thinkers and tinkerers. They need time to transition and consider what you are considering. This man has a biting problem. And it's his problem, not the Grey's. We worked together on his movement and transition habits, for the Grey's sake. He loves that bird, but not enough to honestly admit his attitude is the problem. At our last session he seemed immovable. And that was our last session because without his changing there was no room for fixing the issue; his issue.

I think on that companion often to this day. They are both experiencing far less of a relationship than they should be, only because the human in the room isn't able to be honest with himself. But from the first meeting I held little hope. His opinion was the bird had a problem that needed fixing, not him. Knowing thyself is a two part job. You will need to know and honestly acknowledge what you know. Without that last part of acknowledgment change is impossible. And success will be out of reach for both you and your companion. There's a very easy way to discover your true self. This reflective exercise lets you not only be honest about who you are but acknowledge the truth of the matter. Because the evidence was literally built by yourself.

Reflective exercise includes looking at your friends list. We are a reflection of our friends. Without any thought to the process humans collect and build human networks that best reflect, support and declare their own belief systems. We are the company we keep. Do you consider your circle of friends to be patient? Do you see them as thoughtful? Do you see them as empathetic with great listening skills? It may seem a bit odd, but honestly finding ourselves is simply seeing the truth of who we invite into our life. Your friends, their habits and interplay in your daily life and free time plays a very big part in expressing your true self.

Consider how you spend your time and money. Your time and your money are an honest evaluation of your value system. In fact, how you use your time and your money says more about you than your friends list. Your time and money investments tell everything we really may not want to admit, too. These two commodities are brutal truths. How do you invest your time and your money? Are you an experience hunter? Spending your money and time to experience the world around you? Given to spontaneous travels or experiences? Or do you siphon those two commodities into creating a "nest" at home? Building and filling a sanctuary for yourself and a close set of family and friends. Obviously the latter is parrot preferred.

Companion Parrots require routines. They require routines that deliver expected results consistently. By consistently I mean more than 80% of the time. None of us or our lives are perfectly tuned. But the majority results must defer to successful routines and expectations. Because through these successfully run routines Companion Parrots are able to build trust into their environment, their flock and their relationship with you. Consider wild flocks of simple song birds. You'll soon see they live on a schedule. They show up at certain times for foraging in your backyard. Look and watch close into that event, you'll see the same cast of characters sharing and negotiating parts of your backyard in almost the same choreography every day. Parrots are the same in these instincts. A parrot does very well in a home where routine exists delivering clear communication that needs will be met, all flock members are present or soon to be home, and all is well and healthy inside the flock. Sincerity and routine are invaluable lifestyle characteristics for success.

Ironically a parrot can change, modify, accept and grow into most anything you change, modify, accept and grow into with him/her. You choose a parrot that fits who you and your life are now, and changes are no longer a problem. He's part of a flock. When a parrot feels safe, secure and part of the group, group changes are a simple thing. Group routines and schedules can be modified successfully if you and your Companion Parrot do the modifying together while remnant routines are still in existence. Forget the romantic idea of changing to meet a bird's requirements because you "just want" a cockatoo (for example). I promise you the odds are VERY low, lottery type low, that you can change everything that needs to change to meet the needs of an inappropriate parrot lifestyle choice. Sincerely know yourself first, and I promise finding the perfect parrot companion will be easy. And the lifestyle you both create, share and modify together will be successful.

Chapter 2
They require nothing less than our Sincerity

I keep three books on my desk at all times, The Art of War, the Zen Doctrine of No-Mind, and the Art of Happiness at Work. I have all three for one reason. Sincerity. These books remind me to be sincere in planning, living and working. Sincerity is the key to living a happy life. It is the key to creating a happy lifestyle and it is absolutely mandatory for creating a Successful Companion Parrot Lifestyle.

Parrots are completely sincere. Humans are, for the most part, not sincere. A parrot can never learn to be insincere, but a human learns how to be insincere early in life. Insincerity is part of the rationalization skills we use to negotiate life in social settings. We learn how to answer a question enough to stay out of trouble, but not honestly enough to show our true nature or selves. In a small way we use insincerity to protect ourselves from being, appearing or feeling vulnerable. Sincerity is not the act of being truthful, it is an act of honesty.

You can be truthful and not honest. I can ask you what the sky looks like, you can state the sky is blue, that is a truth. But to be honest you would add that you also see deep grey clouds building from an approaching storm. The devil truly is in the details, or lack thereof.

Insincerity has been so fined tuned in today's society it is rarely called insincere. So you see it's up to us to make this happen. And why wouldn't we want to be sincere? Why wouldn't we want to be sincerely honestly happy? It's a very simple process, it only gets complicated when you allow the chatter of the world to lie to you. Deep thoughts. But deep thoughts make big strides.

A parrot will sincerely want to chew a couch. We react with an insincere question, "Why are you chewing the couch?" As if we are expecting our companion to offer an explanation to their attempts at chewing our couch. We know better. There is no why with parrots, not human whys anyway. They are not misbehaving. They are not being a bad parrot. They most certainly are not being insincere about this attempt. They honestly want to chomp on our woodwork.

Our parrots are chewing on items in their environment because they can, and because they must and because that is what parrots do. They chew on all things interesting in their environments. And they are sincere about doing it. It is our attempt at applying a human cause and effect to that chewing that is the insincerity in the room. And it's our attempt at putting a human wrapper on a parrot piece of logic that will lead to miscommunication and unreasonable expectations. Insincerity creates unreasonable expectations. All parrots chew on furniture, woodwork, things and humanly inappropriate household goods, at least once. Maybe twice if the first time was satisfying. Most likely a third time if you didn't give them a good reason not to try that third time. And that is the honest truth.

The sincerely honest reaction to a parrot chewing on a couch is simply walking over to your companion and requesting a step up with a simple instruction. "Be good." Notice I suggest "Be good." not "Stop that." "No Chewing!" or the like. I suggest stating the honestly sincere hope we have from the situation. We do want them to be good. A positively worded instruction leaves a clear differentiated phrase. There is no getting confused between what to do and what not to do.

After your positively sincere and honest request place your sincere parrot on a location of better choice. Their cage top with a chew or foraging toy waiting for them there. And finally sincerely let them know they are good, you are pleased and here is where you both can share a moment that your companion will seek out again. "Be good." just took on the meaning of sharing time and toy with you.

Sincerity is simple. Human rationalization and debate just mucks up the works. Our parrots sincerely do not want to "challenge" us, or "test us" or provocatively "push our buttons". That is a human wrapper of insincerity. Our companions want what they want because they can. And if we continue to insincerely approach these moments they will quickly assimilate the interaction as a result. And you will be peeling your parrot off your window blinds many times a day.

It is not easy to be a sincere human in this world. But we can make this a new character trait not only for our own personal success but for a sincere result in the relationships with our parrots and family members.

You may have a Companion Parrot that wants nothing to do with a human in your home. At least that is how things seem. But whether there is interaction with the person or no, that person sincerely affects your Companion Parrot. And I will venture to say that parrot's rejection sincerely affects the human. Nobody enjoys being rejected. Every parrot and every person in a home affects the flock mentality no matter the amount of interaction. I've helped many a flock by simply pointing out the individual in the room that seems least impactful to the whole. You can have 2 companion parrots in the same home that never really interact at all. And yet their simple presence sincerely means something to each other. The same can be said with the humans in the room. The emotional health and contentment of the human(s) in the room directly affect the companion parrots in the room and vice a verse.

Insincerity is a weed. We aren't born insincere. If anything we are all born blunt as butter knives honest. Ask a 3 year old if the outfit you are wearing makes you look fat, you'll get the blunt side of that knife every time.

We learn to hide truths through seeds of experiences. We learn to fabricate ideas, reasons and methods by watching others grow their own insincerity weeds. And over time we forget the simplest of things. Being happy is very difficult when we are busy wanting more stuff, comparing our lives to others, realizing our teeth aren't as white as they could be, and generally spending time insincerely building reasons why we are not measuring up to an imaginary but present insincere ruler. I call it First World Disease. If you access advertising, you are mainlining insincerity. Period. I know, I worked in advertising. If you access provocative television programming you are mainlining insincerity. If you choose to spend your time looking over the fence at the grass on that side, you are literally growing insincerity weeds on your side. To live sincerely is to live fully aware of simple truths. Our companion parrots simply want to be, and they simply want to be with us. We can muck that up pretty easy with complicated insincere attempts at being like, acting like, or buying like the next parrot flock.

It is a sincere truth when I say any flock governed by a person of love, patience, sincerity and empathy is a successful flock. I don't have to look at your home. I do not have to take inventory of your food supply, toy supply, cages or schedule. Because love, patience, sincerity and empathy exist. And all good things follow from those qualities.

Here's the thing about a Successful Companion Parrot Lifestyle; you really need to be a successful person first. And by that I mean a sincere, happy, empathetic person. Forget behavior modification for your parrots, and consider that for yourself first. I do. I am happier for it, too. The best part of creating that successful lifestyle for your companion parrot are the side effects produced for everyone around you. Maybe we can all become kinder to each other. Maybe we can all realize the validity of all life, simply. Maybe we can forget our whitening toothpaste for a few minutes and think about helping our neighbor in need. That's where this success leads us. It leads us to sincere living. Quite frankly, I think parrots could save the world.

Chapter 3
Reasonable vs. Unreasonable Expectations

I have a strong tendency to bring unreasonable expectations to my work. Call it my Achilles heel. I honestly fall asleep every night looking forward to the next day and all the exciting results of my efforts from the current day. I expect big things to come every night. It's totally unreasonable in the real world, and can, over time, cause frustration for me. I haven't decided if I'm a positive thinker or arrogant, but there you have it. I fight unreasonable expectation every day. Expecting too much always leads to my feeling stressed. Oddly I have no expectations of the unreasonable type for our Companion Parrots. They are parrots, and I expect the unexpected. I am rarely if ever stressed with or about my Companion Parrots.

Stress is born of expectation. Frustrated stress is born of unreasonable expectation. What is the biggest influence in your parrot's health and the well-being of your companion lifestyle? Unreasonable expectations and the stress it will produce. There is not enough room, food, flight, or toys (employment opportunities) to overcome unreasonable expectations and the stress it breeds. Stress starts with us. We affect the tenor, vibes, energy and environment more than any other element.

At every parrot visit I attend, and in every parrot problem I consult all misunderstandings start with the human in the room. It's a change required by the person, not the parrot. Most fixes are so simple that when I reveal the issue, it's just a big "OH!" in the room and changes are made immediately. And results show just as fast. And in all cases we find ourselves agreeing that an expectation first thought reasonable, was not. And at that very moment of conception it created stress between the parrot and human in the room. A Successful Companion Parrot Lifestyle starts and ends with a relaxed, patient and confident human in the room. There's a difference between simple and easy. These two words are mutually exclusive in context. Sharing your world with a Companion Parrot is simple. It is not easy.

It's the expectations we create in our heads for and toward our relationship with our parrot that can make the simple, difficult. It is the control of that human nature that is truly not easy.

The foundation of success begins with reasonable expectation defined by honest evaluation of ourselves. You cannot want a Macaw and a perfectly kept and well decorated home at the same time. The macaw will lose in that situation. You cannot be a workaholic, gone 10-12 hours a day, and have a Cockatoo. Being honest about who you are, and what you are capable of accepting inside your own truth allows reasonable expectation, and that allows success.

The simple truth of a Companion Parrot is that the daily care, food and routines required are not complicated. Knowing the absolute truth on needs and adding reasonable expectations allows success. Oh sure, you can get all caught up with conversations about nutritional needs, sun lamps vs sun light, feather care and baths and what products you need. You can fuss over vitamins and symptoms of lack of vitamins etc. and so on. You can get fired up on what to clean with, how to clean and hygiene theory. Searching the internet for answers can get you running down rabbit trails of worry and concern. Which leads to unreasonable expectations that lead to stress, which bleeds to your parrot. Which isn't necessary.

Reasonable expectation toward a Companion Parrot cannot include the idea of easy. Because the conversation must include a parrot's expectations. And parrot expectations inside a human world generally seem unreasonable. Chewing on your favorite chair seems reasonable to a parrot. Wandering on the floor to find where you went off to, and chewing on random things while searching for you, is reasonable to a parrot. Companion parrots are not easy because of their expectations to their world. That's the nugget at the center of the truth of expectations for both parrot and human.

It is the parrot's expectations that get overlooked when we find ourselves in a moment or situation that seems troublesome. Bad bird, bad behavior, unwanted behavior, misbehaving, mean bird, unfriendly bird, all these phrases drive me up a tree. I'm up a tree because when a few minutes of conversation takes place it is always revealed that the human brought unreasonable expectations to a parrot's natural expectations and the two do not connect. By default the parrot is found guilty simply for not thinking and acting like a human. The human having passed judgment sees nothing but a faulty bird that needs fixing.

Meanwhile back inside the bird's brain, he's already forgotten about the issue and moved onto another matter, or chair to chew on. That's the other half of parrot expectation. They do not linger in thought. If things get difficult or their chosen path is blocked they just change the subject and goal. Just like a 4 year old child. You, Judge Human, are now alone in your moment of judgment and irritation.

The "screaming parrot" issue is a prime example of unreasonable expectations on the part of humans. With a Vet visit and a parrot being confirmed healthy and not in pain a screaming parrot is acting most appropriately inside their reasonable expectations. They are seeking their prime directive. Flock activity. Every parrot is different and requires a different level of "togetherness". Understanding your parrot's definition of this expectation allows you to fulfill it properly and thus ends the screaming. This is not easy. This is simple. That is the Art of the FlockCall.

As I sit here on the couch with my laptop appropriately sitting on its namesake, editing and rewriting this chapter, I have 8 uncaged parrots within just a few feet of me, including one on my head. They all have chosen their version of comfort roosted, perched, shredding, gruxing, eating or preening. It is so quiet in this house I can hear the wind against the window pane and the blue jays complaining outside.

Why? Every parrot's flock activity level requirement has been met. This was not easy. It took months of repetition, modification, and changes to discover each companion's preferred routine. But going through the modifications was simple. I removed unreasonable expectations, allowed theirs to reveal themselves, and modified my requirements to meet them in the middle. I can work 4 hours straight in the morning in complete quiet with no interruptions from 2 macaws, Felix, Kirby the IRN and 4 cockatiels free to roam and do their thing. I can, after a shared lunch break together, continue this work habit in the afternoon. I don't say this to brag, it's simply a case of allowing a parrot's expectations to show the way.

Some negotiations came into play. (No you can't have my Wacom Pen Butters. No you cannot sit on the monitor Snickers.) That is the part that is not easy. How not easy? The negotiations for not sitting on my monitor required my husband to build a complete open faced cabinet to house that monitor.

Butters and I have come to terms with her needing to be on top of the cabinet when it's time to urge me to take a break. She'll fly over, land, look down on me and say "HI!"

Which to her way of communication is simply stating the obvious. She needs my time to hold her, talk to her while preening her head in front of her favorite window while singing quietly to her, for about an hour. Yes she needs this time, she requires this routine to know all is well in her world and to allow her to communicate her devotion to me. Because you see, a companion parrot derives much joy from being allowed to love us back. And many a parrot will learn the words I Love You. And those companions may well use those words in their time of adoration. You should accept them literally and deeply. The trick to finding and creating these moments is reasonable expectation. Not an easy task some times. But mandatory to allow the time to notice the small suggestions and invitations our companion parrots will bring to us every day. Reasonable expectations allow a fluidity in life. Unreasonable expectations cause us to force things in an effort to get that mandated expected end. We are so focused on what we wanted, we miss what we could have had freely.

Chapter 4
The Value of Time

Time has lost its true meaning since technology brought the microwave, cellphones, and the Internet. There are cultures in the world that were built around the respect and admiration of time and the investment of it. Master creators, religious leaders, artisans, writers, philosophers, star gazers and inventors all embraced the sweat of the brow over time to create meaningful ideas, relationships and items. Time was once understood as an important and mandatory element for creating important and meaningful change. Time was once important. Now time is considered a threat, a stress. Something to quicken, shorten, spend less of and save. Time has few respecters, but many manipulators and detractors. But the truth of its value has not changed. It still exists. Time still yields greatness to those who invest theirs properly into all matters of life experiences.
I am here to tell you creating a successful companion parrot lifestyle and relationship takes time. A lifetime of time.

I have a collection of bonsai trees. I've had them over ten years now. Which is only 20% of the time I've walked this planet. I'm particularly proud of two trees. They started as one. I found an ornamental Ficus Benjamina in a garden center. When it was young the grower wound it's trunk around a length of bamboo to force it to grow in a spiral shape. The trick is, you have to change out that bamboo in yearly intervals, and care for the trunk to keep it healthy in that unnatural growth pattern. That did not happen to this tree. It was left to forge its growth around and into that bamboo. By the width of the trunk and size I'd say I brought this tree home at about 10 years of age or better. It was also close to dead. Its leaves were full of mites, what leaves were left. But its trunk was strong, and the nebari (root system above the soil) told me it had a chance. There were signs of health and there were signs of promise. I'm all about underdogs, and honoring the struggle to live. And I am most definitely all about signs of promise. I live in a state of perpetual promising thought. So much like Charlie Brown and his little Christmas tree, I took this Ficus home.

It took a year to bring this tree back. I removed the bamboo trunk piece, removed the infested leaves, watered and fed this tree back to health. The second year I decided to take the top of the tree and create a second tree from that separation. There's a way to do that, it's a normal practice in bonsai. Not to belabor the story with details I successfully separated the green canopy and heavily twisted trunk. The trunk regrew a whole new canopy system. The bottom grew into a brilliant canopy structure as well. It took 9 years to end up with two brilliant bonsai trees from one abused near death, unwanted, and stuck in the discount corner of the garden center tree.

I have bonsai trees for a reason. They remind me every day that there is no such thing as a microwave minute in life. Microwave minutes belong in the kitchen. Life isn't about the end, it's about the time spent inside the journey. Our companion parrots require us to remember this truth. Because their lifespan can be as long as a human's, and they do not wear watches. Your companion does not care what time it is, and they are uninterested in your human schedule needs. Companion Parrots just do, as long as they feel the joy to do.

I have had many a human ask "How long will it take before my bird can (insert requirement here)?"

My answer; "I can't say. We'll have to wait for your companion to let us know."

Relationships require time. Somewhere relationship time value was lost as well. I will blame the Internet and online dating services for the perversion of healthy relationship practices and the sincere and serious effort and time they require. Great relationships require unconditional time investment with reasonable expectations.

Snickers has been a handful since he fledged. He's a scarlet macaw, we knew in the beginning what was coming our way. We also knew that with patient empathetic communication he would get through the bossy, nippy, biting, pushy male scarlet into a great companion. We knew we would receive exactly what we gave. We've been investing for 3 years in Snickers. He's growing up into an amazing boy. Loving, silly, humorous and so attached to dad that his willingness to choose me so openly is overwhelming. We've built routines for him to thrive inside. He has times for flight, rowdiness, wrestling, sharing, napping, playing tricks and defining his space. Yes, we allow him to be the boss inside routines setup for that attitude. He is a scarlet macaw, and must be allowed to define his space and permissions; it's in his DNA to do it. Going through year three we are literally reaping all the sowing of the last 2 and some years. When we first brought him home, still young and not fledged, we carried no expectations on behavior growth. We didn't write down benchmarks for Snickers to meet. We just met him in the middle with understanding. We offer Snickers routines that openly allow him to be that male scarlet macaw.

There's a simple secret to helping a parrot understand our ideas of acceptable. It is this; you go first. You as the human in the room must first understand a parrot's idea of acceptable. You must accommodate the reality of having a companion parrot first. This accommodation creates reasonable expectations that create positive moments between companion and human. Truly there is no such thing as a bad bird. Truly when a companion parrot is acting like a parrot, rather than a "pet", you are experiencing the reality of the lifestyle not behavior issues.

Like a bonsai tree, you are in the moment working for the future. You can't short change the process. This journey with a companion parrot, large or small, is best enjoyed in the now. If you pay attention to the now, you'll notice the changes more readily, and you'll notice something that is so much more precious than the finish line. You will see them *trying*. Moreover, at that moment of trying to be good or trying to talk, trying to share, or trying to achieve with you your relationship blossoms in strength. You'll feel it. It can be overwhelming. Great relationships should be overwhelming in the heart. That is what makes them great.

Chapter 5
Routines create the Lifestyle

Routines are more than just scheduling bullet points so all can stay on the same page of life. With companion parrots, routine is a very powerful tool that can funnel focus, interest, expectations and attention to the things and actions you hope to promote and grow inside your companion parrot lifestyle. Routines set unspoken truth, expectations, and understandings without saying a word. Creating purposeful routines and delivering expectations inside them remove large sums of behavior misunderstandings between companion and human. Routines make more sense to a companion parrot for communication than "behavior modification" training. Bribing a companion is a humans' idea of reward. It makes sense to a human. We work for a living. Humans learn that life is about reward systems. From birth to our deathbed, we do things for rewards. From employment to shopping online, our choices are driven by gain of reward. It only makes sad sense that humans decided reward systems will work for companions, fur or feather.

I find reward systems in the human dynamic as insulting as I do inside the companion parrot lifestyle. It is insulting to the hearts and minds involved. A full life is lived beyond just rewards and into the rewarding. And although derivative in language these two words do not mean the same thing. Companion parrots and humans are quite alike inside the idea of rewarding. We as humans want to be needed, valuable to others, impactful and heard. Frankly, parrots want the same thing inside their flock.

Given a choice between a walnut and helping me fold clothes, all my companions would prefer my project, the flock setting and me. Every time. I don't bribe with food. I give choices. Our routines offer moments of choices for all. Our Macaws prefer flock, Kirby likes individual results. And all will choose their cage time willingly during the day because the introduction routine lets them know they will be enjoying autonomous play with company still nearby. They know it is a moment containing naps and privacy while I am around cleaning. Or writing. Or a few other creative projects I've worked into these routines and expectations.

A flock desires and requires balance, peace, calm and understanding. Wild flocks do not bribe each other inside the group. There is a synergy that requires a balanced effort to please and receive pleasure inside flock needs. Companion Parrots do not need to bribery because they are not looking for bribes. They are looking for balance and communication, they are looking for materials, location, flock and food in consistent and peaceful routines that all proclaim the same truth. You are safe. You are loved. You are in your flock. When you take the time to create routines that deliver clear road signs of time and expectations, the only behavior issues will be those of the human's unreasonable expectations. Which is great. You can fix those behavior issues yourself.

Routines cannot come from thin air, or be understood right off the bat. Much like my bonsai trees, routines have to be built, modified and strengthened over multiple times to set the direction and gain the outcome. Setting a good routine starts by locating and identifying two sides of the equation; the need and the companion's natural action. Understanding why you want a routine begins the process. I spend roughly 6 hours a day writing and creating graphics. Four hours in the morning, two in the afternoon. I write late into the night, but the birds are asleep, and a routine for them is unnecessary. How does one use a computer, Wacom tablet, laptop, cellphone and the like with 8 flying parrots using 100% of their free choice? I set expectations through routines.

The birds and I have built a very clear identifiable routine I do not deviate from Monday through Friday. Every step tells every member their flock responsibility, my expectation and their choices inside the variations.

The routine as it plays out over 4 hours allows choice for all within routine expectations. I can use my technology without issue during this time. I can think, type, move, walk away from my desk to get more coffee and when I return, all companions are exactly where I left them. Because the routine stayed clear and within their expectations of results. You see, a routine is a two way street. Companion parrots can bring their expectations to the routine as well. Moreover, they have a right to expect us to live up to theirs. Many times humans have the idea that behavior is strictly the Companion Parrot's responsibility. That cannot be further from the truth.

Balance requires both sides to meet equally in weight and action.

For clarity, let's take a walk through a morning to see the choreography of routines for my house. First things first, which is Felix. Routine starts with sound in our home. Felix is listening for Dad to get up. Once he hears dad in the morning we are all off to the races. We've built in a routine that until Dad uncovers him he won't be uncovered. I don't bother uncovering Felix, because he has zero expectations for me. He doesn't want me until dad leaves for the day. So my getting Felix up is a routine breaker. He becomes frustrated looking past me and for dad. I stay out of it Monday through Friday.

While Felix is calling for Dad with a happy voice of "Good Morning Felix!" the others are stretching, preening and slowly waking for their day. They know that it is mom who gets them up for the day. They have no expectations for Dad whatsoever. So the voice, sounds and interactions of Felix and Dad mean only one thing to them; soon, but not now. This results in not a peep from the rest of the flock while Dad and Felix do their morning routine. Dad comes downstairs with Felix. We all say goodbye and Dad heads out. The routine changes. Now Felix looks to me for breakfast. I ask him if he wants some breakfast. Felix answers with lip smacking sounds and a happy "Apple popcorn?"
The rest of the crew upstairs remains silent. It hasn't been 12 hours of dark, and they know it. The next routine is my logging into my computer, coffee in hand, and answering emails and messages. The flock upstairs can hear me typing. They know the routine. I work for 30 minutes.

Felix finishes breakfast and wants his tent covered tree stand, with him on top, rolled into the office to the right of my workstation. His routine changes here. Now he needs to keep me under surveillance. This also means that soon I will be going to get the rest of the flock. With the rolling wheels on the hardwood floor, they know it. I park Felix. Kirby is the first to flock call down the stairs with expectation. I will honor his righteous expectation immediately. We have an understanding.

Routines based on time and actions can transition through sounds. Felix hears Dad. Felix expects Dad. Felix sees Dad leave, hears the garage door, or the motorcycle start and Felix looks to me with expectation for the next step. He is expecting breakfast. If I try to feed the dogs first, it is I with the behavior issues. Our human daily lives are signals we barely recognize outwardly, but like Pavlov's Dog, we react instinctively. Companion Parrots seek signals for communication. The beauty of routines is harnessing our natural signals and defining them for our companions through met expectations and repetition. Felix and I barely speak in the morning. Not because we do not love each other, but because we so understand each other's routines, words just are not necessary. Granted he does love the bit about breakfast. Our lifestyle is defined through routines. Whom we bring into them, what we do with them, and the goals we create by utilizing routines all define our lifestyle. They are the fiber of our day and the cloth of our value system. Successful routine planning and usage creates a successful life.

The magic of routines, the super power of routines is they are adjustable gears that fine-tune our lifestyle for even more success.

Chapter 6
Lifestyles Create the Relationship

I chose the word lifestyle years ago to describe the truth of companion parrots. Bringing such an independent, flying, intelligent, free thinking, problem solving creature into your human domain requires acknowledging that this is a lifestyle choice, not a pet idea. Approaching life with a parrot with any less awareness will cause more frustration than you might imagine.

Their lifespan, intelligence and ability to create a strong mental connection with their human flock offer a meaningful friendship. As a mom, I find their relationship as deep as one forged with a young child. These feathered children communicate through multiple channels we normally do not utilize. They will not grow up or out of the house. They are capable of learning as much as you will teach. They are completely self-aware and motivated by that awareness. With these facts in hand it's obvious that parrots are companions requiring a full menu of emotional investment and not a pet that will only require substantive care and housing. Treat a companion parrot as a pet and you will witness a slow degradation of mental and physical health unfold.

Companion parrots bring their own expectations, needs, and requirements and unlike any other companion, they make themselves loud and clear when we are failing. If our lifestyle is not living up to the requirements necessary to meet their emotional and physical needs, we will find ourselves with problems not easily understood or unraveled. I have worked with a number of these types of flocks. It is heartbreaking to see a companion cut off from clear communication. Unable to make themselves clear because the human in the room has lost their way with the relationship and the lifestyle. It does not have to be this way, ever. Companion parrots are not complicated. They are hard work. Like a good marriage, a best friendship, or family relationships. You will have to actively invest yourself into the relationship. And you will have to do it sincerely, consistently and meaningfully. All that being said; if you've not created the lifestyle through established routines of communication all those possible disconnects become even more difficult. Which is why companion parrots are the fastest growing segment of rescue animals today.

A successful lifestyle for you and your companion parrot depends on you, not the companion. There is no looking to a parrot to cooperate with a bad idea or choice. Parrots aren't built to tolerate things that are unfamiliar, threatening (by definition that is unfamiliar), or shocking. I think on a client that brought a greenwing macaw into a bad lifestyle situation. Her choice, although filled with good intentions, was set for failure. She wanted to rescue this particular macaw from a bad situation; her emotional choice overlooked the problems waiting to happen.

She lived in an apartment. Which isn't necessarily an issue, but in apartments if your companion is making their normal flock calls your neighbors may take exception. She lived in an apartment with a son aged 17 who was beyond angry at the world and into the realm of arrogant rage. During my visit, his hostility filled the apartment. I could feel the stress when I walked in. This boy was cold and unwelcoming to me. Through some seated conversation with his mother, I learned she had never had a parrot before. She had problems with her son and his friends that came in unannounced. She worked long hours as a single mom. The bird was in a huge octagonal cage with no toys, one perch, and one rope. She had no idea how to truly care for him, but she sincerely wanted to fix things. The things needing fixed were enormous, immovable, and slightly dangerous. She asked me what to do to make this bird stop lunging, stop trying to bite, start being nice and stop yelling during the day. I quizzed her about routines for and with this parrot. There weren't too many, as her schedule was so tight and unforgiving. Her son was disinterested in the bird and refused to even help feed him. There was nowhere to go with her and for this parrot because there were no routines to build off to recreate a proper lifestyle.

Routines are stepping stones to successful travels back to balance inside a flock. Even just two routines, morning and night, offer toe holds to build from in creating lifestyle change and improvements. Alas, her greenwing had nowhere to step except away from there by joining an experienced flock family that included another greenwing.

Your lifestyle is the stage where you will build the relationship with your companion.

Your lifestyle will either accommodate growth or it will choke it off. By simple definition, a successful lifestyle is identifiable, manageable and modifiable routines that yield consistent results. However, before you think, "Oh Great! My life is crazy! You should see my schedule." consider you are considering your schedule. What is a schedule but routines attached to time management. Which carries the banner just as well. A busier person will want to consider a different type of companion than a stay at home person. I do believe there is a companion for just about everyone. I truly do. The key is the simple definition stated above.

A stable environment that offers sanctuary and a sense of absolute home is a great lifestyles start. I do not judge a home environment by finances. Castle or hut is irrelevant to the value. The value lies in the stability of home, and the ability to maintain that stability.

FlockCall has a global presence and working with partners around the world the word stability has its variations. And ownership of land and home falls into a wide gap of definition due to governmental controls and socio-economic influences. Working globally has enriched my perspective, experience and understanding of what successful companion parrot lifestyles can be and are today. Many companion parrot rescues will not rehome a parrot to renters. Some find this offensive. Personally, as one who just recently bought a first home, I think rent verses own is a very individual situation.

Generalizing is dangerous footing. We rented one residence for over 10 years to save money and stay in one location for our children's school years. No, stability has less to do with money or ownership as much as it does with the heart and mindful focus of the human in that home. A stable home is a setting that is filled with dedication, focused love and routines created to support that environment. The human in the room is focused on creating a sanctuary of safety and comfort. Stable home is just another form of love. There is a sense of ownership to the life that occupies the space.

The foundation of a successful lifestyle is stability in a home occupied by life expressed in love, pride and commitment. Overlooking the foundation doesn't work.

Rationalizing current issues, whether personal or financial, does not change the fact that the foundation is shaky. You can build a very wonky house of cards on a solid foundation. When helping with flock problems, I find a good percentage of causation ends up inside the foundation of a home.

Something or someone slipped and the home is no longer offering love, pride or commitment. Stability was lost under a pressure. I spend more time talking with the human in the room than ever interacting with their companions. In fact, helping companion parrot flocks doesn't require a face to beak meeting. It only requires a face to face.

265 or so flocks into my personal advocacy and it's been this way on every occasion. This is where the magic of companion parrots shine through. They are a mirror to what is right and what is wrong in us. Which is a grand thing indeed. Creating your successful lifestyle will literally create a successful you as a human. You have no choice but to improve or eliminate bad habits, bad choices, things and people that are not adding success to your life. Creating this lifestyle will make you a stronger person. Creating this lifestyle has made me a stronger person.

I am not a morning person. Over all my years I've built up a lifestyle to support that preference. I built up such a great and powerful lifestyle for it that I had become quite the grouch when the sun came up. Imagine, being grouchy getting up early to get on your boat to go fishing early in the morning in the Gulf of Mexico. Yes, I was getting up grouchy! How very sad. And how very weak of my character not to appreciate that opportunity and ability. I was acting against my own best life interest and actually causing disappointment for my husband. Where was Felix in all this? Well, he was roosting in my Art Studio at that time. We thought he would prefer the quiet and privacy. I look back at that now and realize I just made that up. I did not want him waking me up early. I did what any good and proper human does to get what they selfishly want and I rationalized that tale of privacy needs. And so for about a year Felix woke up early and I didn't wake up early until forced. That is a broken companion parrot lifestyle.

I am not sure where my epiphany came from when I brought Felix into the Master Bedroom to roost with us all. But I do remember feeling guilty. And I think that guilt started when Felix would say "Good MORNING Felix!" and throw a kiss even though he had to wait on me. I think Felix painstakingly revealed this truth to me over time. Now of course we have him in the Master, and he wakes up as early as Dad gets up. He calls out good morning, but doesn't want me Monday thru Friday. He wants Dad. Saturday and Sunday are a different matter. But I'll get to all of those routine details in a later chapter. It took Felix 3 months to get us straightened out. I do get up early now. I get up early with a smile and I am actually happy to do so. Felix and I have a closer relationship for early mornings. He does look for me to say good morning. I think my husband is glad to have a morning person as well.

I trust our companions for their input. Companions are hyper sensitive, some more than others. They can pick up on human stress, anger, fear and anxiety more than a dog or cat. Our companion parrots are not domesticated animals. They've not been assimilated into the human dynamic because they have one super power that we can never possess. Flight. It is the ability to fly that has caused their elevated sense of self. And rightly so, I would love to be able to fly! And I'm pretty sure I'd be one confident woman if I could. Companions are vigilant and sensitive creatures in the wild and inside the human dynamic. It keeps them healthy and alive. A stable home environment is tantamount to all other successful steps because that state of calm and certainty sends a direct line of communication to their vigilance that all is well. Whether you are bringing in a new parrot, or 30 years on into a relationship, all parrots literally "take in" their environment.

When leaving one room for another, watch your companion's reaction. They land, flock call or perch still. There is a transition moment where they are taking full inventory of items, people, emotions and status. It may only last a second, but parrots are continually triaging their environments for change. If a parrot is brought into a stressful environment, like the greenwing example I mentioned earlier in the chapter, they will literally shut down any further influences. They will bite, lunge, rear up, call loudly, and make a serious effort to get you to stop whatever you think you are doing and leave them alone. They are on high alert, they are defensive and unsettled. They are unsure. Problems will be caused by this, and problems will be hidden by this and problems will be multiplied by this issue.

Recently I was asked for help with a very defensive conure. Six years this companion had been with his human, since fledging. And now he was biting, attacking, screeching and downright angry. His human had had a perfect relationship with this conure until recently. We talked quite some time about her bird. The answers I was getting weren't making sense. I knew something changed in this parrot's environment and lifestyle. But the answers weren't revealing. His human preferred to talk about the relationship lost, not what changed. And then a breakthrough in the story telling! The bird had been attacked by their dog. That attack changed everything for the bird's lifestyle and routines, not the dog.

This companion lost his cage to a new cage put into a new location. They bought a new larger cage to compensate for being in a room alone. That in and of itself shows a human rationalization applied to a parrot's needs. Which is always a recipe for failure. The parrot was left in such a position he could only see people by a reflection in a mirror, rather than direct sight. Mirror reflections and light waves being bounced can play havoc with a parrot brain. This parrot was used to being in the center of the action all day long. His cage was posted literally to watch every one come and go through the front door. His lifestyle had been front and center and knee deep in the flock actions. Now he could only hear such comings and goings. His frustration was so great he would fly out of his new room, find his favored human, perch on her shoulder and then bite her ear or neck and fly off. His frustration was clear. All his routines, his lifestyle and his literal home were turned upside down. He didn't give a hoot about that dog. He healed well and was healthy and beyond the incident. The human in the room was not. She was worried for the safety of her companion. And rightly so. But had approached it through an emotional set of human beliefs rather than a parrot's instinct and perspective.

The lifestyle fix was obvious; get the old cage back in place. Leave the new cage where it was. Get a doggie gate to keep the dog permanently out of the parrot area. 36 hours later she had her loving companion just as he had always been. She called it magic. I called it stability. This companion parrot gained a new play area as a bonus. Now that he had his confidence and home back he adopted the new cage and it's location as a secondary favored spot. Happy as a clam to nap and play hide and seek. Which reveals another truth, parrots are quite flexible inside a stable and happy flock. You can count on a companion parrot to accept quite a bit of transitioning if it is done inside a routine, with repetitive steps that they can recognize. Much like building a bridge. They'll go anywhere with you, if you take them through familiar routines via transitioning introductions. That last bit requires leaning on the relationship built between you and your flock through routine, stability, time, sincere communication, and rational expectations. A companion parrot requires the same building blocks as a healthy human relationship. These things don't happen over night. You will have good days and some bad days. But if you love someone, those things are expected, forgiven and celebrated as growth within your relationship.

Chapter 7
Relationships create communication

You do want a relationship with your companion parrot. Because seeking that relationship requires a line of communication and trust to be built. When I say we should seek a relationship, some will say "Oh yes my parrot and I are very bonded". I'd like to strengthen the definition of both these terms inside the successful companion parrot lifestyle for clarity. One of the major problems with companion parrot rights and being understood is the language we use in reference to them. Poorly defined words coupled with misuse can cause confusion which creates unreasonable expectations for humans.

The word "bonded' gets thrown around in the bird world. I suppose because it's origin started with breeders referring to two parrots who are inseparable and have chosen each other as partners for breeding. Bonded isn't really the right word for a human/parrot relationship though. There will be time spans where your companion will change their mind about you and them. You will loose your shoulder buddy, your love bug, your snuggle bean or your travel partner. They will literally wake up one day and shut you out of all those normal moments you expect. Because it's a fluid relationship between a human and a parrot. We aren't bonded as a parental pair of companion parrots that lasts a lifetime. The commitment isn't to breed to ensure the species drive. It's important to understand this truth. No matter the status of your relationship now. You may be thinking; "Kathy you should see my relationship! We ARE bonded!" I would not argue the commitment of your relationship, but I will reiterate this is not bonding.

This is a wonderful example of a loving stable and committed friendship and love. That will ebb and flow and change and come back again. Because that's what a relationship is between a human and a parrot. We do not bond with our companion parrots. We do grow with them inside a deeper relationship if we put the effort in, as with any relationship. And in understanding this truth, we can reasonably expect there may be temporary or long term opinions about us by our companions. It is a natural occurrence.

Every parrot is an individual, like a human. Each relationship and flock have their own abiding truth for themselves. But there are a few threads of truth that all successful flocks share without exception. Empathy is one.

Empathy is the simple act of understanding the feelings and nature of another. To empathize with a companion parrot is simply always being aware of their perspective. It takes a bit of creative thinking, but just look at a moment from their perspective. A great example that I'm called in to "fix" is the need for a companion to call out randomly. Some more than others. And some louder than others. I call it flock calling, others call it screaming, screeching or bad behavior. Empathetically speaking though, it is just a bird doing a status check. That's it. Flock calling is a natural and necessary practice for all parrots. And the fact that it's loud inside a house or apartment is irrelevant. This has to be done and it needs to be answered, by you.

Parrots are in a constant state of assessment. They have to be. Nature has taught their kind that they must know who's who and where's who all the time, or somebody is going to get eaten. Parrots flock. Parrots are group event creature. Groups need communication to stay in a group. Parrots need assessment and communication constantly. How many of us shout across our house to locate a husband, child or wife? (I know I do!) So why are we expecting our Companion Parrot to be quiet?

You are part of their flock. You must be located and communicated with constantly. So why aren't you answering the flock call? Flock calling is a great game of Marco Polo and logistical communications. Parrots thrive on it, parrots desire it, and parrots who get that feedback tend to be MUCH quieter parrots. Because over countless flock calling events you, the flock member, have always answered. So your parrot trusts you, and your parrot is less anxious because you are a good flock member.

There's your empathetic understanding of a companion parrot. Next time your parrot(s) are making a ruckus, call out their name. Do it again. Listen to their call back. Soon it will be a game of Marco Polo and I guarantee they will love it.

Try calling first when the house is quiet. Just call out their name. Listen to their call back. This is another form of bonding and trust building. Because everyone likes to feel needed. And everyone likes to feel part of a group. That's empathetic action. The thing about empathy in a parrot/human relationship is it will have to be practiced by you, not them. Which isn't to say your companion will not emotionally empathize with you, they will learn when you are sad, happy, sick, frustrated and such. And in a healthy relationship they will react accordingly. Felix, our African Grey, never fails to notice when I am stressed about something. His response is always the same. He simply tells me, "It's all right!" He's never been wrong about that either.

Active Patience is another thread running the length of a successful companion parrot relationship. Patience on our part must come first. Active Patience is a constant state of being.

We've an exotic companion and their perspective and ways tend to require us to patiently empathize and patiently react to all kinds of actions on their part. We need to literally apply an active state of patience to our day and our relationship. Which is challenging in as much as that requires time. Lots of unconditional, free flowing, empathetic reasonable expectation time.

I have a collection of bonsai trees. I've had them over ten years now. I'm particularly proud of two trees. They started as one. I found an ornamental Ficus Benjamina in a garden center. When it was young the grower had spiraled it's trunk around a length of bamboo to force it to grow in that spiral shape. The trick is, you have to change out that bamboo in yearly intervals, and care for the trunk to keep it healthy in that unnatural growth pattern. That did not happen to this tree. It was left to forge it's growth around and into that bamboo. By the width of the trunk and it's size I'd say I brought this tree home at about 10 years of age or better. It was also close to dead. It's leaves were full of mites, what leaves were left. But it's trunk was strong, and it's nebari (root system above the soil) told me it had a chance. There were signs of health and there were signs of promise. I'm all about underdogs, and honoring the struggle to live.

Talk with your parrot! Notice I didn't say talk to, I said talk with your parrot to include and wait for responses. A conversation is only as good as the listening that goes on. Give your bird a chance to respond, whether it be a ruffle, or vocalization or a head shake or a toy toss. Listening is as important as talking with your parrot. Parrots communicate through body language, vocalization and human speech. They take what they learn, and what you've learned from them to build a very personal communication route just for the two of you. You will literally build a new language with your parrot, and that building can only take place if you are together sharing parts of the day and thoughts.

Share food with your parrot! Seriously. Share a meal with your parrot. Why do we go out to dinner with friends? For the shear enjoyment of eating together. You laugh, share stories, try each other's foods, you bond. What parrot won't like that? Food for companions is as powerful a tool as any other in building understanding.

Let your parrot help with chores! Okay, this is a bit wishy washy, but riding on a pile of laundry counts as helping. The point being, a parrot needs to be part of the daily dailies. They need that. Snickers helps with dried laundry by pulling everything out of my basket and throwing it on the floor. He's not messing up my work, he is literally helping. He waits for me to pick things up and fold them before he gets the next item. Snickers loves throwing clean clothes on the floor OR in his perspective; helping me fold laundry. Shared goals is a powerful force for human and companion. Shared success creates trust and joy.

Flock call with your parrot! Are you outside doing lawn work? Are they in the house? Well, yell hello into the window! It doesn't have to be open. Wave, sing, dance. Hide behind the bush and play peekaboo. Are you in the other room busy? Call out and let them know you are safe and near, and busy. Every body appreciates updates. Being together for a parrot isn't just proximity. Voice and calls are just as valid to a parrot as sitting on your shoulder. Of course a close knit companionship will create the preference to be with or on you rather than just hear from you. Some parrots can become quite attached. Which isn't a bad thing if you've ever had a parrot purr in your ear, you'll become quickly addicted. Always speak a word to your parrot when walking past their cage or line of sight. Always. Nobody likes being ignored.

Say hello and goodbye during your day's ins and outs. Nobody likes being forgotten. Acknowledging change of flock formation is imperative. They know you are coming or going. By creating a routine of hello and goodbyes companions left for a trip, work or an hour are far more relaxed knowing you are coming back, because you always do. You promise it through action, and prove it through completion. Parrots keep track of all you say and do and compile those experiences as part of their communication catalogue.

Say their names, often. Parrots LOVE hearing their names. It's true.

If they love snuggling, snuggle. If they love scritches, scritch. If they love rolling around on a bed and wing rubs, well do it. Felix isn't a snuggler at all. He's a thinker. BUT he appreciates dad's head and face rubs. Snickers requires bedtime snuggles, wing rubs, belly rubs and foot rubs with dad. This is not an option. Butters loves head, chest and foot rubs. Anytime she can corner me. I could spend hours standing in front of her favorite window pouring love on top of her like hot fudge. She'll just purr like a cat. I know someone will warn of the dangers of physical touch to certain areas (the back). I know someone will stand opposed on this issue because of hormones et al. And in some cases that is a true warning. SOME CASES.

Every bird is different, every lifestyle is different and every companion parrot relationship is different. Do not fear or push away a physically welcoming parrot. Yes, I have had a parrot rub me in a mating way. Both he and I were left unsatisfied and it didn't happen again. Bottom line; enjoy your parrot in that snuggle and petting sense that works for you both because it works and brings joy and calm. It just makes me sad to think there are flocks literally denying their relationship this level of discourse because of a perceived unknown. Balance, as with all things, is the answer. Treat your parrot no less than you would treat a child or friend. Literally. If for no other reason than to make yourself a better and kinder personal naturally.

Chapter 8
Communication creates personal growth

Acknowledging the inherent changes and lifestyle modifications that will happen by including a companion parrot into your life is a necessary step. Some changes and accommodations will give you pause. Others will cause your non parrot friends to scratch their heads. But in the end, it's no different than bringing home a brand new baby. Your goals, focus and loyalties change at that very moment.

It is to be expected that your nature and your own habits will change with every day that passes with your companion parrot. I know this applies to our flock and me. Somewhere along the line these last few years the parrot's eating habits became mine. I generally stray away from dairy and meats anyway, and I'm not a fan of sugar. So maybe it didn't "become", so much as just slip into line. At any rate, there it is, I eat like a bird.

I've also taken on odd table habits while eating. I catch myself at restaurants guarding my plate and piling all the condiments, cutlery, napkins and loose items into a defensive corner. Oddly children in the vicinity don't even bat an eye. Their parents seem to linger in their glances attempting to make sense of the fort of items while wondering where my kids are at.

I've also taken on habit while dining out to order for the parrot's leftovers more so than for my dinner. I read menus with a parrot brain. I consider what I can eat, so I can bring something home to them. I suppose that's just a translation from grocery store habits. I am looking for food. I order meals and ask for things to have things on the side of things, so as not to mix things in objectionable manners. Felix really doesn't like his broccoli perverted by any other foods. So, I need mine served in a separate bowl. Waitresses love me, they need a serving platter stand, and 3 assistants to bring out my meals.

Grocery shopping has taken on a whole new meaning since our flock emerged. I normally make a list and know 95% of the trip will be spent in the produce section. The other 5% is in the pasta isle. Fresh produce and pastas make up half the nutrition and calories I feed the flock.

I rely on parrot specific mixes to deliver the nuts, seeds and pellets. Pellets make up about 20% of the total. I'm not a big fan of them and do not look to them to deliver the bulk of nutrition. As you can see I'm totally aware of the parrots needs. But again, I'm not giving self awareness a thought. I've got bigger fish to fry. Or broil. The parrots love mackerel.

I try to leave for shopping around 1-ish. I hate putting every birdy in their cages earlier than that, and I try to get back by 3. They shouldn't be locked up too long. When buying real estate with parrots in the family, try to make sure all your shopping needs are within a mile. It helps. Additionally, if you can, try not to worry about what you look like at any given time. I've gotten really good at that last part. Self awareness has melted away a little at a time with every new parrot taken in.

And so, with my trusty phone, list saved to it's memory, I head out to the store. Mental notes running through my head not to forget that I may need to pick up a few things for myself and husband to eat. But whatever, I'll deal with that later. I wonder if I changed completely out of pajamas into street clothes. Probably, if not, whatever. Did I brush my hair before putting it up? It feels like it. I suppose I should have looked in the mirror before going out in public, but whatever. I needed to look in the bird pantry and see the status of things. There's only so much time for awareness, and that self thing is overrated.

Thankfully, Kirby assisted in my list making and pantry inventorying this morning. Faithful as always, he sat on my head and buzzed and chattered and let me know he was a good boy, and needed more flax seed. Very helpful little guy.

Park in the back of all the parking lots when shopping as well. Taking a walk to the store doors gives you more time to ponder what you may be forgetting. Many a time that 100 meters gave me the moment I needed to realize I'd forgotten to swap slippers for street shoes and that Butters is almost out of her favourite dates. You can stop right there and put that on your list, or in your phone. Don't worry about the slippers, no one will notice.

I've found starting at the produce section gets my mind right on target. When looking through fresh items, don't be afraid to pick up a few and really look at their color, skins and flesh.

Additionally, when shopping groupings of greenery, remember the latest additions are in the back of the groupings. You'll have to pull some out of the way, and there will be a few other shoppers gawking at you for the mining you are doing in the fresh lettuces, but whatever. This is a parrot mission. Check those expiration dates on boxed, pre-washed lettuces as well. Again, you'll have to dig back into the display to get the best expiration date. Don't mind the other shoppers staring at you. I don't.

The bright and more colorful the greens and fruits, the healthier they are, so really get in there and dig around those displays of apples and oranges, pears and kiwis, plums and prunes and pick the best and brightest. The employees will gawk too, probably annoyed with your messing up their complex geometric stacks of fruit. But whatever. Oranges weren't built to create pyramids with anyway.

Some days you garner more gawkers than others. I sure did this day. Obviously they were either impressed with my committed shopping behaviour or possibly the quality of foods in my cart or they just couldn't understand how brilliant my strategy was, in either case I was not wearing slippers! I had that going for me.

Timing is everything they say, and just about the time I pulled up in the driveway, home again, my husband pulled up as well. Early day for him it seems, which means I have some help to bring the results of my genius into the house! We are both greeted at the door with "Hello!" "Hi!" "Snickers!" "WHAT?" "What are you doing" and Felix's ambulance noises. It's good to be home.

Cali and I take the first trip of bags into the house together, side by side. So romantic and domestic. With a smile and a chuckle my beloved husband gawks at me.

"Where'd you go today, honey?" he asks. So sweet, to be interested in my adventures in public.

"Oh, the usual, Target, Publix, PetSmart and the Dry Cleaners." I say, proud of the accomplishments.

He opens the door for me to walk in first. We put the first group of bags on the counter. He stops, I stop, we gaze into each other's eyes, thankful for each other and our life. Parrot songs and chatter of happiness, our soundtrack.

"Baby", he says, as he reaches out to push some hair away from my face.

"Ya?" I reply.

"You have Kirby Poop all over your head." He laughs and walks out to the truck to finish bringing in the genius that is my shopping.

"Ya, well whatever!" I shout over my shoulder, "I'm not wearing slippers!" Which brings up another lifestyle modification; wardrobe needs.

I shop for clothes thinking of my parrots, too. I can't wear thin material around the house, Kirby snags his little claws on shirts like that. I can't wear clothes with patterns, baubles, glitter, sparkles, buttons, bows, bright graphics or patches either. My wardrobe consists of white and black T Shirts basically. My "in the home" wardrobe is four times larger than my "out of the house" wardrobe, too. Parrots churn and chew and shred shoulder areas and collars and seams. I suppose I could get them to stop that, but hey, it's part of their preening me, and that's quite nice. I don't mind. Most of my "in the home" wardrobe comes from thrift stores. I'm not investing in retail numbers here. And besides, nothing says bodacious bird mom like a T Shirt that says "Keep on Truck'n" with a big foot walking toward you.

I paint murals on our walls. Yes, I am an artist, and it tends to be expected I'll do something like that anyway. But in practicality, a parrot can not throw a mural off a wall like a framed picture. Oh, sure they can lick it maybe, but I'm not Willy Wonka and that's not Snozberry flavored. So they tend to ignore the art as an object. I've painted paintings of paintings on the wall. Which is hilarious! Butters still can't quite get over the fact there really is no edge to grab and pull on. Keeps her busy.

We have multiple sets of measuring cups and spoons in our kitchen. Well actually, we have an eclectic collection of mismatched and chewed on, bent and dented measuring cups.

I don't cook, I don't care. Parrots are fabulous assistants in the kitchen, if you lower your expectations about dinner.
Inclusion seems like an assumed result. Bringing companions into the home will include them into the lifestyle. That inclusion will bring about some interesting changes for you, them, and the household itself. One of the trickiest inclusion issues that rears it's head in the companion parrot lifestyle is today's tendency toward divided attention. Humans are an easily distracted breed. Most of us humans understand, if not embrace, the new divided attention of humanity. Who hasn't had a walking conversation while checking a cell phone. Some choose the virtual reality of gaming to reality. Slicing up their days by 8 hour patches of virtual combat or movie themed war. We may sit in the same room with the gamers, but in the end, we are alone. Their attention is divided, and they aren't even aware of that division. We get together only to have some visitors scrolling their cell phone while talking with us. They are with us, but not totally.

Our new society of divided attention is normal to humans. Personally, I don't like it. I have been known to ignore my phone, or leave it behind. I don't do selfies and I don't carry it in my hand when out and about. It is my purse for communication needs. And those needs are pretty strict. Ask my kids. "WHY DON'T YOU ANSWER YOUR PHONE!?!" I get that often.

Companion Parrots do not understand divided attention. At. All. For a companion, it is frustrating, and impossible to understand. Parrots do not live a life of undivided attention. They are fully connected and fully aware of themselves, their world and those they love. Our parrots murder our cell phones, controllers and other buttony communication devices, keyboards and computer mouse for a simple reason. It divides our attention, and they know it. Why should they appreciate that? They don't. It is the thing that removes the communication they thrive on.

As with all parrot issues I've worked with and around, the issues start with the human in the room. Divided attention is either the root of the cause, or the root of inability to identify the cause at all.

There is no auto pilot for parrots. There is no half hearted living with a companion parrot. There is no parrot that is a pet. Companion parrots are not complicated. Parrots are hard. They are hard because parrots do not rationalize one thing in their lives. And they certainly won't understand why you've left to talk on a cellphone. Which is why when that cell rings, your companion may start flock calling like mad. This isn't a game, it's an attempt to stop the divided attention.

Snickers our scarlet macaw has a fabulous technique when we think we are getting away with serving him divided attention. He flies at the bathroom door off the main birdroom, lands as hard and loud as he can, and hangs off the frame with one foot. He chews on the frame, climbs on the door with the loose foot and looks at us. If we continue in our act of divided attention he will modify that and fly over to a window and hang off the horizontal blinds. All this is our fault. He is after all, just communicating. Message received Snickers!

Yes, we as the humans are pulled in all directions. Some directions are out of our control, some because we just want that direction. But we didn't buy a pet when we brought home our companions. We made a lifestyle choice. And this lifestyle requires practicing undivided attention with our companions. It's no different than a 3 year old, who has gotten really good at running and controlling their physical choices. You can't successfully share your life with a fully mobile and choice driven toddler utilizing divided attention. You can't really build a successful relationship either. Even if the Christmas cellphone commercials tell you otherwise.

When you are with your companions, be with your companions fully. It's a small statement that yields huge success.

Chapter 9
Fully aware communication creates the success

A successful lifestyle consists of sincerity, invested time, reasonable expectations, supportive routines and honest evaluation of our selves and shared experiences. Consider this a recipe for both you and your flock. With this recipe you will create the most powerful element of any relationship; great communication.

Communication with a parrot is an Immersive event. Parrots communicate in multi-dimensions; Sight, touch, sound, spatial recognition, temperature, light, atmosphere, flock member metrics, and irregular feedbacks to name a few. Humans, thanks to social evolution, generally communicate in two; Sight and sound.

Communication between parrots and their human flock occur on uneven ground. And that's where problems can start. Expanding our communication between the flock goes a long way in helping issues improve and keeping issues from starting all together. I will use the Grey Parrot as an example, but for all intents and purposes these ideas and suggestions are applicable across the whole companion parrot spectrum.

Greys are thinkers. They are not neurotic. I find the word neurotic difficult to hear and would really love to see it removed from Grey conversation. It's a human word. It's not a parrot word. Greys are thinkers and tinkerers. They are communicators in 4D and prioritize their judgments toward us and their items and their surroundings in that manner. Greys can be slow to no to accept things. This is not neurotic. This is a Grey.

Immersive Communication and layered messaging for our parrots sounds overwhelming, but it's no more difficult than planning a party. And you can plan this party for any parrot, and every parrot will benefit.

When we find a companion our first goal is to parrot proof our home. Which is advisable, no doubt. There are things that need to physically change for their safety. I would like to also suggest the next step needs to be parrot promoting your home as well. When we learn we'll have guests coming over, or in-laws what's the first thing we do besides clean the bathroom? Pretty much set the house up for people to enjoy. We get the rooms and backyard ready to show off and show fun for our visitors. Why? Because everything they see, hear, smell, touch, taste and feel will affect their visit. So, we already have an instinctive understanding about parrot promoting through our entertaining instinct, we just need to tune into the parrot mindset as well as our goals for a lifestyle with our companion parrot. Because everything we bring to and around our bird WILL send a message. And those messages need to be synergistic with our words and requests.

After you've made your lifestyle choices, create your immersive communications around that decision. If you are not a cook and you do not enjoy cooking, then don't kid yourself that you'll be making birdie bread every Saturday. If you are particular about your home, don't assume a fully flighted macaw will be a great companion decision. Let's apply immersive communication and lifestyle decisions to the touch stones of a parrot/human communication:

Food and parrot nutrition is a personal, passion filled, and at times confusing subject. Bring up the subject of food and your parrot and you'll find yourself in the center of some serious claims, warnings, recipes, and adamant beliefs. Food is personal, very personal. So let's approach healthy feeding practices along the same lines as any other companion lifestyle subject, with simple facts and balanced ideas that allow personal viewpoints and choices.

I approach healthy foods and feeding from the perspective of foraging and simplicity. This benefits the budget as well as the companion parrot. Consider your companion from the native wild side. Google up some searches on their wild cousins and what foods they eat. I'll just use Felix as an example for this thought. Being an African Grey, the foods profile tends toward leaves, bark, young plant growth, snails, available nuts, seeds and flowering fruits. Simple enough. Or how about Kirby our Indian Ringneck Parakeet extraordinaire! Seeds, grasses, young flowering growth, vegetation, flowers, the occasional bug.

What every parrot has in common in the wild they have in common in the companion setting; food is not only about eating but about employment and work. There are no bowls in the wild. There are no chopped anything waiting for easy consumption. One of the lost arts, or maybe it was never really an art, is feeding our companions for employment's sake. Bowls are great, chop is awesome and laying out banquets of organics is a wonderful thing. But let's remember that companion parrots enjoy the process of eating and discovering things to eat. It's in their DNA as much as flight.

Chop is a fabulous idea. It's trending hard and strong in the companion world. Chop delivers in the parental satisfaction category. Who wouldn't be proud and feel good about serving chop to their parrots. It's full of nutrition and delicious. Chop is a great idea all in all. Chop doesn't work in my flock though. No one appreciates it. I used to offer it once or twice as week as an addition but it was always left behind. So I went back to offering the same items in larger formats, in foraging ways and laid out as the whole food for the macaws. Felix loves chopped apple, but he hates chop with apple. Chop is a great gateway food. Powerful in transitioning a parrot off cheap seeds and into the realm of healthy eating as well. But chop has some downfalls.

Chop completely bypasses the need for a parrot to work for their dinner, to forage, and to explore. Chop masks texture, flavor and identity of foods as well. Most chop failures occur because of these three points. The finer the chop, the harder it is to identify what is being offered. Flavors mix to create one profile of pulps, which can turn off some parrots. Apple doesn't taste like apple and romaine doesn't taste like romaine. And yes, I do believe parrots taste food. Chop that is frozen and thawed, will immediately begin to degrade and breakdown. The nutritional values and structure loss speeds up in the decomp processes once it hits the oxygen in the air. If they don't get in it or on it within the hour things get mushy. That's great if a parrot likes mush, but if not, all that frozen chop just lost it's appeal. Extreme chop, with many components tend to create a situation where the odds go up in rejection because the reject-able items were increased. And you'll never know what the offense was because of the mixed flavor, texture and item profile. So many variables to turn a parrot off are there and so many are left to cypher for the parent.

Don't get me wrong, I'm not saying chop is bad. I am saying chop, like any other companion idea has it's good and bad points to consider inside your flock. The best practice for chop; keep it simple and under 4 items. Keeping the items short listed allows you to cypher what wasn't working and remove that one offender. Or you can limit the chop to a family of foods; lettuces, fruits, green veggies etc. Again, this will allow a taste profile that is easily cyphered. Keep it fresh and created the day of serving. The very component of chop, food being chopped up, makes freezing it's Achilles heal.

What of pellets? I like to keep our pellet ratio at less than 20% offered, which, after rejection to the floor leaves about 10% consumed. Read the label. If your pellet's first ingredients are anything related to corn, wheat or soy, understand those ingredients are GMO affected. Without fail. These are the least expensive way to create the binder for vitamins and fats. That's why it's used. It is the same process for dry dog foods. Check for sugars. They'll be in there under their copious naming. Look hard for it. You don't want empty calories. Consider the vitamin profiles. If you can't pronounce the vitamin origin names, then you may want to pull out an apple instead. Pellets are processed foods. Organic, holistic or no, they are processed, so find that brand that provides the simplest format of ingredients and find that balance. There are good products that walk the mid-ground of provisions. You'll give up something to get another in pellets. I do suggest reading the labels and consider how you are going to provide nutritionally dense calories. And consider how you will offset what the pellets aren't giving your bird with wholefoods. Personally, I lean heavy on whole foods, dried fruits, raw nuts, high value seeds, then pellet mixes. And yes, we share our dinners as well.

Foraging and dinner time. Skewering fruits and veggies, placing bowls of foods in different places, wrapping morsels in foraging papers, boxes and toys, and simply handing a big parrot an apple are all legitimate avenues. For the record I do not fear apple seeds, the data doesn't support the fear. Unless you are offering a couple tablespoons of apple seeds a day, and they eat every one, it's just a non starter of a food fear. Our macaws love being handed a whole cucumber, mandarin orange, apple, summer squash, winter squash etc. I let them figure it out. That's the idea of it. Smaller parrots need smaller options, cut in half or quarter or just miniature sized. Whole sweet peppers are a hit across the board in our flock.

What about imported foods from other countries? Pesticides and differing laws globally make things tricky to be sure. Are grapes from Chili dangerous? Specifically Chili? I don't know. I purchase grapes as local as possible and when necessary I do buy dark grapes from Chili. From a local major grocery store. I know grocery vendors differ from grocery store to grocery store according to price point. I do know that buying local and small grower works out better than big box and cheap trucked in. I do know some foods are no longer even grown in the US due to many reasons. Food is changing and where and how it is produced is no longer decided by the nutritional value, but on the cost per kilo and profit per shipment. Food is a commodity and only judged as the dollar value left over from the business expense. Quinoa is a trendy new grain. But as of yet, no one has asked how the grain is grown, where or what pesticides are used to gain it's market share. Palm Oil was the big thing for a while, until it was revealed palm oil demand is leading to the destruction of native parrot habitats. Ironic isn't it. Food is personal on many different levels.

You do not have to spend hundreds of dollars and hours of time to successfully nurture and feed your companion parrots. You do not have to stress and worry about food origin if you keep it simple, fresh and local. Don't ever feel you aren't living up to your parrot's food needs because you can't afford the time or money for kale or quinoa. Good old broccoli, apples, almonds and flax seeds, veggie pasta and such get the job done just as well. Food and feeding our parrots is supposed to be enjoyable and gratifying and a shared moment of kindness. Simple, balanced and informed leaves lots of time for that happy moment your parrot grabs the food right off your fork or chooses to share their morsel with you by dropping it on your head or down your shirt. I find that very gratifying.

Location settings offer visual communication. Creating a larger visual environment around a parrot's cage, will have an exponential effect for a parrot's comfort. There's a reason we buy homes with lots of windows. And there's a reason we decorate our home with things we love, art that speaks to us, and photos that remind us of those that are important to us. That same visual environment is required for our parrots. If you are house proud, or a "Martha Stewart" home creator, you may want to double think the idea of a parrot. You have to give up ground to them. You have to marry yourself to the idea that they need a free range area or areas that are parrotriffic, not HGTV designed.

Interior design rarely says, "put that furniture right in front of the window so you can't see the view." But parrot design says, "put the cage in front of the window so THEY can see the view. You won't see as much of course."

Visual environmental design is a simple but thoroughly creative process. If your windows are small, or you just can not put the cage right in front of them for a reason of comfort, traffic or vents, there are a number of other solutions that are just as powerful. Near a window with line of sight and visual environmental design cues can really do the trick.

Some know I have painted all the walls in our downstairs area with murals of natural scenes. Mangroves, intercoastal waterways, palm trees and Floridian underbrush. I painted a tree canopy on one ceiling above a large tree stand that is positioned directly under it. These are environments. They aren't real, and I do not think the flock believes otherwise, but they add a visual difference. Something to ponder. A feeling as well. Snickers' favorite spot in the whole house is under the Tree Canopy ceiling next to the mangrove painted wall, top of the tree stand. He reaches up and tongues the leaves at times. Any time of the day, he prefers there. Kirby prefers right in front of a window if he has to be in his cage. Butters prefers the brightly lit bird room with palms over 40 feet of wall.

Offering visual environments in different locations as well as near or in front of their cage is a vitality generating move. Parrots need choices. They thrive in a choice based world. Given choices, a parrot is stimulated, thinking and exploring. Giving defined choices takes that parrot to a controlled stimulating, thinking and exploring place. Parrots wonder and get into trouble when they are bored, or when their place has become less than an area you have setup for yourself. Which takes us back to giving ground up to your bird. You define your rules by the environment you create.

Don't expect a parrot to find a tree stand with one hanging toy and a bowl of something to trump a stack of magazines with a TV remote on top. That tree stand will loose that contest. Never expect a parrot to behave well in a home not parrot proofed for their way of thinking. It is unreasonable, and unfair.

BUT, let's say you create a tree stand inside a visual environment described as follows: You have the tree stand positioned near or in front of another window, outside is a bird feeder for viewing. The tree stand itself has multiple perches creating a 2 or 3 story climbing event with toys, and foraging bits and crumpled newspaper with nuts stuffed inside. There's a bell that rings whenever your parrot pulls on a rope full of straws cut up and tied up. The bell is hidden, so they haven't discovered where it is yet. They have to figure that one out. On the wall behind the tree stand in a shadow box you've hung. In the shadow box is a picture of them!

Now compare that to your magazines.   Of course you put the remote away. No one leaves a remote out in full view if they have parrots. And those stacked magazines just became invisible comparatively speaking.

A view starts with a window, but it is so much more than that. Take a walk through a Kindergarten classroom. You'll find colors, shapes, objects stacked, bright pictures on the wall, blankets and carpets full of color and pictures. I have a rug for children that has a picture of a town on it, so that the child can drive his toy car around. Butters and Snickers love that rug. I buy big oversized Lego like toys for them. They love those blocks. I put the blocks on the rug and soft jingly baby toys as well. They fly back and forth up and back from the tops of their cages playing on the rug and gathering up the toys to put on top of their cage to play there. Back and forth, up and down. Then they throw everything off, I reorganize and they start all over again.

Materials and toys are another tool for communication. An unemployed parrot is an unhealthy, unhappy and frustrated parrot. I have a hard time bandying the word "toy" around when discussing employment opportunities. The word toy implies a childish activity that is used for distraction. That couldn't be further from the reality. Parrot toys are irreplaceable, mandatory, important and are going to be destroyed. Eventually. Beak and foot manipulation offers mindful thought, exercise to small and large muscle groups, strengthens their respiratory and immune systems, activates creative parrot thought and occupies a very intelligent always running mind. Their need for mental and physical exercise is no different than ours, except they need more of it more often.

Our parrots are driven by three main instinctual drives; location, materials and food. Each of those items leads to other instincts as feeding, mating, play and sheltering. The pointless joy of play has been observed in the wild. They randomize items for the shear silly of it. Location preference is driven by material and food availability. Centralized food and water sources drive sheltering, which brings the girls which creates the flocks and so forth and so on. The complexity of how these things affect a parrot's choice and movement is clear.

In the wild, and in the core instinct of our parrots is the need to constantly be analysing, searching, upgrading, communicating, sharing, building, discarding, compiling, acquiring and procreating in their world. Out there, it's a big world. There's much to consider and even more to investigate. In our companion world, it's much smaller, less is required of them to survive. And yet, they wake up every morning with these instincts that scream, "LET'S GO!"

You can see how a parrot may seem poorly behaved in a human environment. How do they know that rattan chair isn't for nesting and sheltering material? OF course they go into the dog water bowl, it's water! So for quicker typing on my end we'll call toys, **Employment Opportunities**, or EO's for short.

The parrot toy industry has categorized toys for the buyer; foraging, educational, natural, chewing, preening, breaking, refillable, reusable, foot, beak, food and even organic native derived materials toys. The labels tell us what the toy is meant to provide, the parrots tell us what it's really providing. The parrot industry as a whole has one important goal, profit. I don't begrudge that at all, they need to make profit so they can continue and we need them to continue. But what I would like to discuss is the toy peer pressure and guilt. These items are expensive, even with free shipping, or at a discount location. And there is reality behind the packaging I'd like to visit just a little bit. I am an Agent of Balance.

EO's and the amount required is directly impacted by the amount of time your parrot is alone, or in a cage. EO needs are also affected by the parrot's age, and personality. I have met parrots who could care less about EO's, and would rather change locations regularly and ponder the world. I've met parrots who at the age of 4 can not sit still to save themselves. They must always be working on something.

Online shopping and large Parrot Toy Stores are Disney land to most parents. We want to indulge our babies! The color, shape, noise possibilities, size and creations just beg to be brought home. And rightly so. Know your bird before you drop that dollar. Modification through observation! Every time you bring home a foot toy, if your baby throws it on the floor and ignores it, your bird isn't much of a foot toy player. Try taking that rejected foot toy and attach it to an already hanging toy in their cage.

Consider their travels. Do they need to fly with a toy in their foot or beak? My Snickers can not fly without a toy. He is flightless if he has no toy in his beak or foot. Grounded. I keep soft cloth toddler toys for him to grab and fly with, so if he should drop it mid-flight no harm no foul.

What of these new fangled naturally derived native materials toys? Are they better? Well that depends on where and how they came to be, and most importantly how they were handled. What glue was used to get that mass of fun put together? What coloring? Here's the thing, most bird toys were imported before the labelling started about naturally derived blah blah native materials blah blah. Most grass, bamboo, and cork toys were imported in parts and assembled here, or those buyers purchased in mass bulk imported from the Asian markets.

So if you are in an aisle that has a grass toy with no packaging bragging and a grass toy WITH packaging bragging, check the country of origin. Made in the USA isn't a guarantee that the individual elements are from the US, conversely made in China is also not a guarantee the parts were individually derived from China. We are a global community and parrot toys have always been a parts import driven industry. Some materials are not native to the States, and can never be grown here. Better to spend your money by material quality, value of play, metals safety, and design for life expectancy.

Check the wood. There is a hot new trend out there using cork, balsa and soft woods. That's awesome for the little guys, but medium to large parrots will destroy these toys in a matter of minutes. There is soft and hard pine wood for these guys. Look closely at the wood chunks. Where is the grain of the wood going? Think woodworker thoughts. The closer the lines of the wood, the closer that wood came from the heart of the tree.

Heart wood is tough stuff! Know your wood grains. Colored wood isn't necessarily necessary. I used to think I needed the bright stuff to keep them all engaged. I soon learned after my husband got into wood working, and toy building for us, that natural is just peachy keen to all of our flock. It's not mandatory, unless your bird says it is.

Simply stated value of play is the quantity of ways your parrot can play with a toy. They are 4D creatures, monkeys with wings; upside down and right side up! That being said consider hanging toys that offer climbing, hanging, chewing and hiding variables. Parts that offer foot holds, parts that offer an item to hide behind, parts that offer chewing while hanging upside down. WE see a hanging toy as a simple vertical item. THEY see it from all angles and all options. The more the better.

Check that metal! Hooks, rings, and locking mechanisms are generally made of metals. Unless it claims stainless steel, it is not. Watch those elements and when they show deterioration, throw them out.

Life expectancy of EO's is directly related to the sum of it's parts and the sum of the items above. In the end, a toy with a long life could be a toy that wasn't loved in life. (Outside of stainless steel of course.) Expect destruction! Embrace this as a seal of approval, and a job well done by you.

And finally all parrots truly appreciate one toy that is their arch nemesis. THE toy that needs fighting, and conquering every day. You can't shop for this toy specifically, but one day, you will bring one in that is chosen as the coveted "beat it up, smash it up, scream at it" toy. When that EO is chosen, go back and get a couple more. Once an arch nemesis is named, they rarely fall out of favor.

When we slow down, and take the time to reconsider all the avenues and actions that happen throughout a day with our birds, we'll see many opportunities to communicate without saying a word. After all, they are depending on us to understand. They are exotic and not domesticated. We chose them and the lifestyle that goes along with Creating a Successful Companion Parrot Lifestyle.

Successful communication will create a need on the part of your parrot's for more. And in their joy and celebration of being able to talk to and with you they will become loud. It is inevitable.

We all know how quiet the playgrounds are around elementary schools. The children walk out quietly, holding hands, whispering about the slide and swings with cautious thoughtful steps...oh...wait... let's start over.

We all know how quiet public pools are during the summer. Children paddling and floating like waterlilies in Spring...um... wait that's not right.

We all know how quiet a room full of kindergarten children are as they share toys, graciously pass the cookies and milk and wait in a straight line to go to the bathroom...um... hold on...

We all know how quiet children are around the Christmas Tree as they open their brightly colored packages on Christmas morning...it's almost like a Cathedral during mass. Well all that sounds ridiculous! Children are constantly on the move, always looking for adventure and fun. Children are curious and crazy and have little to no editing going on in their head. Why, children are borderline nuts!

So why would anyone expect anything less from their Companion Parrots?

Parrots are in a constant state of assessment. They have to be. Nature has taught their kind that they MUST know who's who and where's who all the time, or somebody is going to get eaten. Parrots flock. Parrots are group event creature. Groups need communication to stay in a group. Parrots need assessment and communication constantly.

How many of us shout across our house to locate a husband, child or wife? (I know I do!) So why are we expecting our Companion Parrot to be quiet?

You are part of their flock. YOU must be located and communicated with constantly. So why aren't you answering the flock call? Flock calling is a great game of Marco Polo and logistical communications. Parrots thrive on it, parrots desire it, and parrots who get that feedback tend to be MUCH quieter parrots. Because over countless flock calling events you, the flock member, have always answered. So, your parrot trusts you, and your parrot is less anxious because you are a good flock member.

You really ought to try this exercise; next time your parrot(s) are making a ruckus, call out their name. Do it again. Listen to their call back. Soon it will be a game of Marco Polo and I guarantee they will love it. Try calling first when the house is quiet. Just call out their name.

Communication as with all our other lifestyle goals requires us to seek improvement whenever possible. Real communication is a skill. The better your communication skills the better your companion parrot and human relationships will be. Being able to share feelings, needs, joys and fears creates a huge amount of trust, for both bird and human. The benefits are the same for both. And they are as powerful.

For the last hour or so I've been standing at the door looking out past the covered deck and into our backyard. I love this view. I love it for the birds outside, our flowered Crepe Myrtle all in pink, my bonsai and plants on the deck and for Butters. Butters, you see, mandates about an hour of time on my right forearm in front of this windowed door looking out. We do this once a day. She doesn't seem to care what time, although prefers the lunch hour. I think she inherited that from my own schedule. I walk away from the computer and she jumps off her tree stand to call dibs.

She wants this hour for one purpose. She must preen my arm, neck, ear and shirt collar. I'm a mess obviously. She carefully, delicately and with a constant purr fixes me. I am a human after all and without feathering I fall short of beauty. She needs this time together. She craves it. It is important to her, it means something to her day and this action between us sends clear communication of our love, her safety and the flock's health.

Every parrot in this house has these Need Times. Some would flippantly call them needy or spoiled. I consider them companions who require their own personal communications between me and them. Little Winston, our male cockatiel, requires about 10 minutes of serious head scritches and neck fluffs every night around 7:30 or 8 pm. I just found out he loves his new name Little Winston. He REALLY likes the word "little". That word and that time tells Little Winston everything he needs to know about himself, us and his flock.

In all the ideas of behaviour, training, controlling and modifying our companions it is imperative to find, create and identity these moments and actions. They are literally the key to success in the bigger format of our companion parrot's physical and mental health.

These actions will take time, and probably a little sacrifice. But then, all relationships require those investments. And like great love affairs, those around us will wonder if we are a bit crazy for it. You know those love affairs. We have all had them at least once. We end up doing some amazing sacrifices for our love. We deny ourselves, we change our schedules, formats and even beliefs! Why we become a different person in the name of love. Some of our friends think us crazy, some think we are making a mistake or even wasting our time. And yet we carry on for our great love. And at the end of the day, very few humans see this emotional overloaded investment for love as unusual. It's expected even.

Step out of a relationship and stay single and watch friends and family "worry" for you. Your mom is going to ask if you are okay alone. Stay single and "alone" long enough with no great love story and then your inner circle may just set you down for an arranged date night. Because everyone should be in love!

I agree, every one should feel and give love. It's part of the human makeup. It is that one thing we all need. It is not something a human can do without really. An unloved person can self destruct. Many an addict, suicide victim or homeless person will voice the feeling of being unlovable or unloved.

Because love is a need that proves purpose. Flocks can not form without purpose.

Flocks and family are first formed through love. And that love creates purpose. And that purpose needs reinforcement and fuel to grow. And Need Time is that fuel. A majority of issues can be wiped out with Need Time. And I mean issues of both parrot and human. Companion Parrots crave Need Time. The best part of Companion Parrots is the best part of Humans. Resiliency when offered love. They, and we, are amazingly resilient when we know we are loved. No matter the relationship issue for a flock, my prescription starts with love. Because we all need love.

Love is the real success found in practicing the Art of the FlockCall. Sincere unconditional love reciprocated between parrot and human eliminates all the problems. You can't buy enough toys, enough organic foods or a big enough cage to replace that element. You can not swap sincere unconditional love with "things" of any type and gain the same successes. That is the bottom line of my Advocacy. You must start with sincere unconditional love and empathy first. Bring that state into your companion parrot lifestyle, and the rest of their needs are met easily without fear.

Follow the Art of the FlockCall and your companion parrot relationship will flourish. Apply these insights to your personal human side of life, and your life will flourish. I'm certain of it. Because I live this Art every day. Love truly conquers all.

Made in the USA
Monee, IL
12 May 2021